COME AWAY WITH ME

A Collection of Original Hymns

Texts by Mary Nelson Keithahn

Tunes by John D. Horman

Abingdon Press
Nashville

Come Away With Me

This book is printed on acid-free, recycled paper.

ISBN 0-687-07272-7

98 99 00 01 02 03 04 05 06 07 — 10 9 8 7 6 5 4 3 2 1

Manufactured in the United States of America

PREFACE

Whether we sing praise choruses or traditional hymns or both, congregational song offers us opportunities to express our faith and explore its meaning as we worship with others in our faith community. Praise choruses, with their simple melodies, brief scripture texts, and emotional appeal, help us "sing praise with the spirit" (1 Cor. 14:15b). Hymns written in a more traditional style, with great concern for theological concepts, biblical references, and poetic metaphors, encourage us to "sing praise with the mind also." While there is a place in worship for each of these approaches, we believe there is also a need for a new kind of congregational song that bridges the gap between "hymns for the heart" and "hymns for the head."

For worship to be meaningful, congregational song should give us opportunities to express our deepest feelings in God's presence. However, the fact that songs of lament and complaint are included in the book of Psalms suggests that praise choruses alone do not satisfy this spiritual need. The songs of God's people must deal with the whole spectrum of human emotions, not just feelings of joy and thanksgiving. When we come to worship we may also be hurting, feeling angry or rejected, grieving a loss, demanding a justice, repenting a sin, or pleading for God's help. We need reassurance that God accepts us and loves us as we are, that we are not alone in our feelings and problems, and that we can depend on God to guide and support us through our faith community. We have tried to address these needs in the hymns we have written for this collection.

Congregational song should also provide opportunities for God to speak to us in worship, giving us new insights and directions for our life as God's people in today's world. The texts of our hymns draw heavily on biblical experiences and faith, offering opportunities for further reflection and discussion. We have provided background information for each hymn as a guide for those who will be teaching and using this collection.

Congregational song should have singable melodies that become part of our tune vocabularies by the time we have sung the third stanza. A good tune is one we find ourselves humming on our way home from worship. It helps us commit a text to memory so that we can retrieve it easily whenever there is a need. A good tune also supports the meaning of a text without overpowering it, and it must be well crafted to stand the test of time. We have tried to provide tunes for this collection that meet these criteria.

Finally, congregational song should be accessible to persons of all ages. The hymns in this collection are appropriate for children to sing as well as for youth and adults. The language is simple, the illustrations are familiar, and the tunes are singable. However, although these hymns are easily learned, they are hymns for all of us to "grow into" as we let God speak to us through the text and tunes.

May the hymns we have written help you sing with the spirit and with the understanding also!

Mary Nelson Keithahn and John D. Horman

CONTENTS

When Quiet Peace Is Shattered

When quiet peace is shattered
by dreadful noise of war,
and we are bruised and battered
by fighting's constant roar,
Lord, break the silence of your word
and let your healing voice be heard.
O let your healing voice be heard.

When troubles still our love-song
and fear beats hard within,
when anger drowns the dove's song
and life's a noisy din,
Lord, break the silence of your word
and let your healing voice be heard.
O let your healing voice be heard.

When clashing wills divide us
and hearts refuse to mend,
when feelings scream inside us
and agonies won't end,
Lord, break the silence of your word
and let your healing voice be heard.
O let your healing voice be heard.

WORDS: Mary Nelson Keithahn
© 1993 Hinshaw Music, Inc.

About the Text and Tune

O God, do not keep silence; do not hold your peace or be still, O God! (Ps. 83:1).

Mary wrote the first two stanzas of "When Quiet Peace Is Shattered" at a hymn-writing workshop led by Carl Daw following the annual conference of the Hymn Society of America at St. Olaf College in July 1991. She added the third stanza at John's request when he set the text as an anthem*. The hymn version is included in *Voices United*, a hymnal published in 1996 by the United Church of Canada.

When Mary wrote this text, she had in mind a disturbing work by Edvard Munch, a late nineteenth-century Norwegian artist. *The Scream* shows a man, wide-eyed with fear. His hands are clamped over his ears to shut out the scream that reverberates from his open mouth and echoes in wavy lines to the four corners of the painting. Whatever the reasons for his agony—the horrors of war, the shock of grief, the frustrations of anger, the hopelessness of unresolved conflicts, the hurt of broken relationships—the noisy din of these overpowering emotions must have made it difficult for him to hear the "still, small voice" of God. Perhaps this is what Helmuth Thielicke meant when he spoke of the "silence of God" during the Nazi years in Germany. It is the silence we experience in the private wars and conflicts that engage us all, leaving us bruised and battered, sometimes literally. It is the silence Mary herself felt when death stilled her love's song and left her to face the future alone as a widow.

God is never silent, of course, but when life becomes so filled with the noise of our anguished feelings, we are unable to hear that "still, small voice." And so we cry out with the psalmist, "O God, do not keep silence; do not hold your peace or be still, O God!" (Ps. 83:1). We long to hear God's voice, because God's Word is Love-in-Action, and when God speaks, healing begins.

John's tune, HEALING VOICE, takes its name from the refrain. It is a gentle, simple tune set on harmonies that occasionally conflict.

"When Quiet Peace Is Shattered" would be appropriate for a healing service, for worship in times of crisis, and for general use.

*"When Quiet Peace Is Shattered," Hinshaw Music, Inc. HMC-1281. SATB with keyboard.

When Quiet Peace Is Shattered

Unison

1. When qui-et peace is shat-tered by dread-ful noise of war, and
2. When trou-bles still our love-song and fear beats hard with-in, when
3. When clash-ing wills div-ide us and hearts re-fuse to mend, when

we are bruised and bat - tered by fight-ing's con-stant roar,
ang - er drowns the dove's song and life's a nois - y din,
feel-ings scream in - side us and a - go - nies won't end,

Refrain

Lord, break the si - lence of your word and let your heal - ing

voice be heard. O let your heal-ing voice be heard.

WORDS: Mary Nelson Keithahn
MUSIC: John D. Horman

HEALING VOICE
76.76 with Refrain

Spirit, Falling Like a Dove

Spirit, falling like a dove,
claim me for the Son of Love,
call me through God's living word,
by the name of Christ, my Lord.

Water, flowing over me,
cleanse, refresh, and set me free,
free to hear God's living word,
free to follow Christ, my Lord.

Spirit, breathe new life in me,
fill my heart that I may be
faithful to God's living word,
friend of Jesus Christ, my Lord.

Spirit, with your fire divine,
seal me with your sacred sign,
mark me with God's living word,
make me one with Christ, my Lord.

WORDS: Mary Nelson Keithahn

© 1995 Abingdon Press

About the Text and Tune

And when Jesus had been baptized, just as he came up from the water, suddenly the heavens were opened to him and he saw the Spirit of God descending like a dove and alighting on him. And a voice from heaven said, "This is my Son, the Beloved, with whom I am well pleased" (Matt. 3:16-17).

Mary wrote "Spirit Falling Like a Dove" in response to John's request for a baptismal anthem text.* John named his tune ENGLISH ORCHARD for the Silver Spring, Maryland street where he lives. This text, which would be suitable for Pentecost as well as baptismal occasions, may also be sung to Ralph Vaughan Williams's tune THE CALL.

The text draws on biblical accounts and symbols of baptism, as follows:

Stanza 1: The dove is a symbol for the Holy Spirit that claims us for the "Son of Love" (Matt. 3:16-17). God's call comes to us through the "living word" (John 1:14; Matt. 6:35; Matt. 4:18-22) and in the name of Jesus.

Stanza 2: Washing is a ritual action in the Bible that makes us "clean" or acceptable to God. It is a sign of repentance, accepting forgiveness, and receiving the gift of the Spirit (Acts 2:38-39).

Stanza 3: John said the one who would follow him would baptize with the Holy Spirit and with fire (Matt. 3:11). The Holy Spirit is symbolized by breath (Gen. 2:7) and wind (Acts 2:2). Jesus called the disciples friends, not servants (John 15:14-16).

Stanza 4: The Holy Spirit here is symbolized by fire (Matt. 3:11; Acts 2:3). Heat is used to apply sealing wax to a document. Baptism sealed the New Covenant just as circumcision had sealed the Old Covenant. The "sacred sign" is the cross that is made on the forehead of the person being baptized. The "mark" of a Christian is Christlike living, a result of letting Christ rule one's life.

---

*"Spirit Falling Like a Dove," Abingdon Press, #503310 (*Church Music for Children* Anthem Series). Unison treble voices, flute (optional), and keyboard.

Spirit, Falling Like a Dove

1. Spir - it, fall - ing like a dove, claim me for the Son of Love, call me through God's liv - ing word, by the name of Christ, my Lord.
2. Wa - ter, flow - ing o - ver me, cleanse, re - fresh, and set me free, free to hear God's liv - ing word, free to fol - low Christ, my Lord.
3. Spir - it, breathe new life in me, fill my heart that I may be faith - ful to God's liv - ing word, friend of Je - sus Christ, my Lord.
4. Spir - it, with your fire di - vine, seal me with your sa - cred sign, mark me with God's liv - ing word, make me one with Christ, my Lord.

WORDS: Mary Nelson Keithahn
MUSIC: John D. Horman

ENGLISH ORCHARD
77.77

There Is a Need for Shepherds

There is a need for shepherds in this place,
where pain and suffering wear a human face;
where hungry children stand outside the door,
and homeless families long for home once more.
There is a need for shepherds in this hour.
There is a need for Love to show its power!

There is a need for shepherds on this street,
where lonely strangers pass and do not meet;*
where hopeless people wander in the night,
and wonder why life never turns out right.
There is a need for shepherds in this hour.
There is a need for Love to show its power!

There is a need for shepherds on this earth,
where young and old have lost their sense of worth;
where guilty people seek to place the blame
on others for their failures and their shame.
There is a need for shepherds in this hour.
There is a need for Love to show its power!

There is a need for shepherds everywhere.
We who have strayed like sheep must learn to care.
We who have known the Shepherd's love today
must shepherd one another in God's Way.
There is a need for shepherds in this hour.
There is a need for Love to show its power!

*The first two lines of this stanza are quoted from "Call for a Shepherd," a poem by Manfred A. Carter that was published in the December 12, 1962 issue of *The Christian Century*.

WORDS: Mary Nelson Keithahn

About the Text and Tune

When they had finished breakfast, Jesus said to Simon Peter, "Simon, son of John, do you love me more than these?" He said to him, "Yes, Lord; you know that I love you." Jesus said to him, "Feed my lambs ... Tend my sheep ... Feed my sheep" (John 21:15-17).

"There Is a Need for Shepherds" was adapted for congregational singing from the last song in *Shepherds Wanted*, a musical drama that we wrote for the 1992 United Church of Christ Music, Art, and Drama camp at Placerville, near Rapid City, South Dakota. During interludes between stanzas, the cast improvised skits to show how Christians can carry on the Good Shepherd's work today. The tune name, SHEPHERDS TODAY, reflects this theme.

The hymn would be especially appropriate for Good Shepherd Sunday (the fourth Sunday of Easter), a service commissioning or recognizing "undershepherds" in the congregation, or at any time when attention is focused on the pastoral role of the church.

There Is a Need for Shepherds

1. There is a need for shep-herds in this place, _____
2. There is a need for shep-herds on this street, _____
3. There is a need for shep-herds on this earth, _____
4. There is a need for shep-herds ev - ery - where. _____

where pain and suf - fering wear a hu - man face; _____
where lone - ly stran - gers pass and do not meet; _____
where young and old have lost their sense of worth; _____
We who have strayed like sheep must learn to care. _____

where hun - gry chil - dren stand out - side the
where hope-less peo - ple wan - der in the
where guilt - y peo - ple seek to place the
We who have known the Shep-herd's love to -

WORDS: Mary Nelson Keithahn
MUSIC: John D. Horman

© 1992, 1997 Abingdon Press

SHEPHERDS TODAY
10 10.10 10 with Refrain

door, _____ and home-less fam-ilies long for home once
night, _____ and won-der why life nev-er turns out
blame _____ on oth-ers for their fail-ures and their
day _____ must shep-herd one an-oth-er in God's

Refrain

more. _____
right. _____ There is a need for shep-herds in this
shame. _____
way. _____

hour. _____ There is a need for Love to show its power! __

Emmanuel, Who Walked Among Us Here

Emmanuel, who walked among us here,
inspiring hope, removing doubt and fear,
your friends are gathered now, so come as you said.
Be known to us in cup and broken bread.
May we walk, may we walk with each other to life's end,
not as servant nor as slave, but as a friend.

As once you walked the Galilean shore,
and voiced a call your friends could not ignore,
draw us to follow in your footsteps today.
Good Teacher, lead us in Love's joyful way.
May we walk, may we walk with each other to life's end,
not as servant nor as slave, but as a friend.

Great Healer, as you walked each dusty lane,
dispensing love to those who suffered pain,
grant us your gentle touch and soft-spoken phrase.
Make us your healing body now, always.
May we walk, may we walk with each other to life's end,
not as servant nor as slave, but as a friend.

Dear Savior, as you walked up Calvary's hill
to suffer there and feel death's awful chill,
when Love demands of us such great sacrifice,
give us your will and heart to pay the price.
May we walk, may we walk with each other to life's end,
not as servant nor as slave, but as a friend.

Lord, as you walked with friends Emmaus way,
and turned their mourning into joy that day,
in us such faith, such hope, such love now increase.
Dear Risen Friend, grant us new life and peace.
May we walk, may we walk with each other to life's end,
not as servant nor as slave, but as a friend.

WORDS: Mary Nelson Keithahn
© 1996, 1997 Abingdon Press

About the Text and Tune

This is my commandment, that you love one another as I have loved you. No one has greater love than this, to lay down one's life for one's friends. You are my friends if you do what I command you. I do not call you servants any longer, because the servant does not know what the master is doing; but I have called you friends, because I have made known to you everything that I have heard from my Father (John 15:12-15).

We wrote an earlier version of "Emmanuel, Who Walked Among Us Here" in memory of those lost to AIDS, and to help Christians affirm and express a living faith to draw on in any time of crisis. The revised text also emphasizes Jesus' concept of friendship as the basis for the covenantal relationships that are so important in the life of God's people. Each hymn stanza develops one aspect of these relationships, noting both the role of Jesus Christ and our call to carry on his work in the world.

Stanza 1 (Emmanuel) recalls the Incarnation, and invokes the presence of Christ as Christians gather again around the Communion table. Eating together is one of the basic expressions of community and friendship in every culture. It is also a time when we learn from one another about the things that are most important in our lives.

Stanza 2 (Teacher) reminds us of the relationship Jesus and his friends had as teacher and disciples, and expresses the hope that we will respond as faithfully to his call to learn from and follow in his way.

Stanza 3 (Healer) remembers Jesus' role in healing the sick, and prays for the gifts that will enable us to be his healing body in the world today.

Stanza 4 (Savior) recognizes Jesus' willingness to share in human pain and suffering, and prays that we will show such love when we are called to make sacrifices for one another.

Stanza 5 (Risen Lord and Friend) recalls the resurrection joy the disciples found on the walk to Emmaus, and asks that we too may find courage, hope, faith, peace, and new life in the knowledge that our Risen Lord and Friend will be with us always.

The Refrain emphasizes that, unlike the servant who puts in time at a job and goes home, or the slave who simply follows orders without question, friends walk through life together, understanding and trying to meet one another's needs. As the loving presence of Jesus Christ is always with us, so we must also be present to one another.

John named his tune KENSINGTON after Kensington, Maryland, the site of Warner Memorial Presbyterian Church where he has served as director of music since 1970.

The hymn is appropriate for Communion or general use. It also offers an opportunity for teaching about the work of Jesus and the church. Each stanza could be illustrated with scenes from Jesus' life and/or contemporary scenes, using pantomime, tableaux, puppets, projected slides (photographs, art masterpieces, or original drawings), banners, or other media. The refrain could be choreographed for dancers.

Emmanuel, Who Walked Among Us Here

1. Em - man - u - el, who walked a - mong us here, in -
2. As once you walked the Gal - i - le - an shore, and
3. Great Heal - er, as you walked each dust - y lane, dis -
4. Dear Sav - ior, as you walked up Cal-v'ry's hill to
5. Lord, as you walked with friends Em - ma - us way, and

spir - ing hope, re - mov - ing doubt and fear, your
voiced a call your friends could not ig - nore, draw
pens - ing love to those who suf - fered pain, grant
suf - fer there and feel death's aw - ful chill, when
turned their mourn-ing in - to joy that day, in

friends are gath - ered now, so come as you
us to fol - low in your foot - steps to -
us your gen - tle touch and soft - spok - en
Love de - mands of us such great sac - ri -
us such faith, such hope, such love now in -

WORDS: Mary Nelson Keithahn
MUSIC: John D. Horman

KENSINGTON
10 10.11 10 with Refrain

© 1996, 1997 Abingdon Press

Duplication without permission is strictly prohibited.

Refrain

said. Be known to us in cup and
day. Good Teach - er, lead us in Love's
phrase. Make us your heal - ing bod - y
fice. Give us your will and heart to
crease. Dear Ris - en Friend, grant us new

bro - ken bread.
joy - ful way.
now, al - ways. May we walk, may we
pay the price.
life and peace.

walk with each oth - er to life's end, not as

ser-vant, nor as slave, but as a friend.

The Kingdom We Inherited

The kingdom we inherited
is not a worldly one.
The realm of Christ is anywhere
God's loving work is done.
His legacy is service to
the least of humankind:
In each needy face, he said,
his own face we will find.

A piece of bread, a saving cup
of water in his name,
a welcome to a stranger,
the healing of the lame,
warm clothing for a naked one,
a visit to the bound:
In each simple act of love
the loving Christ is found.

The kingdom we inherited
is not a worldly one.
The realm of Christ is everywhere
God's loving work is done.
Pray bless us, God, as heirs of Love,
that what we do and say
may reflect the face of Christ
to all we meet today.

WORDS: Mary Nelson Keithahn
© 1995, 1997 Abingdon Press

About the Text and Tune

Jesus answered, "My kingdom is not from this world" (John 18:36a). *"Come ... inherit the kingdom prepared for you ... I was hungry and you gave me food, I was thirsty and you gave me something to drink, I was a stranger and you welcomed me, I was naked and you gave me clothing, I was sick and you took care of me, I was in prison and you visited me ... as you did it to one of the least of these who are members of my family, you did it to me"* (Matt. 25:34-40).

We wrote "The Kingdom We Inherited" for our musical drama, *They Sang a New Song,* to illustrate the compassionate ministry to refugees carried on by Katharina and Matthew Zell in sixteenth-century Strasbourg in response to John 18:36 and Matthew 25:31-44. The tune name comes from Placerville Camp where the musical was first performed at the 1995 M.A.D. (Music, Art, and Drama) Camp.

The text makes use of a paradoxical reverse image of Christ's face. We see Christ in the faces of those in need, and the needy see Christ in us as we offer them our love and help.

The works of mercy mentioned in the second stanza could be interpreted in pantomime or dance as the congregation sings the hymn.

The Kingdom We Inherited

1. The kingdom we inherited is
2. A piece of bread, a saving cup of
3. The kingdom we inherited is

not a worldly one. The
water in his name, a
not a worldly one. The

realm of Christ is anywhere God's
welcome to a stranger, the
realm of Christ is ev'rywhere God's

loving work is done. His
healing of the lame, warm
loving work is done. Pray

WORDS: Mary Nelson Keithahn
MUSIC: John D. Horman

PLACERVILLE
86.86.86.76

leg - a - cy   is   ser - vice   to   the
cloth - ing   for   a   na - ked   one,   a
bless   us,   God,   as   heirs   of   Love,   that

least   of   hu - man - kind;
vis - it   to   the   bound:
what   we   do   and   say

In   each   need - y   face,   he   said,   his
In   each   sim - ple   act   of   love,   the
may   re - flect   the   face   of   Christ   to

own   face   we   will   find.
lov - ing   Christ   is   found.
all   we   meet   to - day.

When the World Is Babbling 'Round Us

When the world is babbling 'round us,
deafening us to human need,
when its selfish ways confound us
as we satisfy our greed,
find us, and free us, O God.

When we fail to hear you call us,
when we turn and run away
until evil times befall us
causing us to stop and pray,
find us, forgive us, O God.

Let your Holy Spirit enter
into hearts on wings of dove.
Let your will be at the center
of our lives afire with love.
Find us, and fill us, O God.

Make us one with Christ in caring
for the outcast and the lost,
that in joyful, selfless sharing
we may never count the cost.
Find us, and form us, O God.

WORDS: Mary Nelson Keithahn
© 1996 Abingdon Press

About the Text and Tune

"Come, let us build ourselves ... a tower ... and let us make a name for ourselves ..."
[God] scattered them ... over the face of all the earth, and they left off building the city. ...
it was called Babel, because there [God] confused the language of all" (Gen. 11:4, 8-9).
When the day of Pentecost had come. ... All of them were filled with the Holy Spirit and
began to speak in other languages, as the Spirit gave them ability" (Acts 2:1-4).

Mary wrote "When the World Is Babbling 'Round Us" to satisfy John's request
for an anthem text for older children that connected the Tower of Babel story
(Gen. 11:1-9) with the event of Pentecost (Acts 2).*

Stanzas 1 and 2 define contemporary "Babel" in terms of the self-centeredness
that gets in the way of our response to the needs of others and God's call until we
need help ourselves.

Stanzas 3 and 4 use metaphors from the Pentecost event (dove, fire) to suggest
what happens when the Holy Spirit enters our lives and rules our hearts.

Each stanza ends with a prayer, beginning "Find us ..."

John named the tune MIDDLETOWN after his hometown in Maryland. The text
may also be sung to BRIDEGROOM.

This is an appropriate prayer hymn for Pentecost and Ordinary Time.

---

*"A Prayer for Pentecost," Abingdon Press, #5002020 *(Church Music for Children* Anthem Series). Unison
treble voices and keyboard, with optional flute or violin.

When the World Is Babbling 'Round Us

1. When the world is bab-bling 'round us, deaf-ening
2. When we fail to hear you call us, when we
3. Let your Ho-ly Spir-it en-ter in-to
4. Make us one with Christ in car-ing for the

us to hu-man need, when its self-ish ways con-
turn and run a-way un-til e-vil times be-
hearts on wings of dove. Let your will be at the
out-cast and the lost, that in joy-ful, self-less

found us as we sa-tis-fy our greed,
fall us caus-ing us to stop and pray,
cen-ter of our lives a-fire with love.
shar-ing we may nev-er count the cost.

WORDS: Mary Nelson Keithahn
MUSIC: John D. Horman

MIDDLETOWN
87.87.7

© 1996, 1997 Abingdon Press

find us, and free us, O God.
find us, for - give us, O God.
Find us, and fill us, O God.
Find us, and form us, O God.

God. Find us, and
God. Find us, for -
God. Find us, and
God. Find us, and

free us, O God.
give us, O God.
fill us, O God.
form us, O God.

The People Came from Everywhere

The people came from everywhere
to hear the Teacher's news.
The blind, the lame, the poor were there,
encouraged by his views.
But those who brought the children near
were quickly sent away:
"The Teacher's far too busy now.
Don't bother him today."

When Jesus saw the children turn,
their faces long and glum,
he told his friends, "When will you learn
that little ones must come?"
He chided them indignantly,
"God's love can't be denied!
Let all the children come to me
and sit here at my side."

"The holy realm of God belongs
to children such as these,
who trust that God will right all wrongs,
forgive, and bring us peace.
If you would also now receive
the love that never ends,
come as a trusting child, believe
in all that God intends."

As once you took your hands and blessed
the children on their way,
now bless us, Jesus, in our quest
to find your love, we pray.
We long to feel your warm embrace,
and hear your kindly word,
that in the presence of your grace
our faith might be assured.

WORDS: Mary Nelson Keithahn
© 1996 Abingdon Press

About the Text and Tune

"Let the little children come to me ... for it is to such as these that the kingdom of God belongs" (Mark 10:14).

In 1995, Warner Presbyterian Church in Kensington, Maryland commissioned Mary to write a hymn in honor of John's 25th anniversary as organist and music director of the congregation, and invited her to preach for the celebration. Because working with children has been a priority for both of us, Mary chose to preach on the story of Jesus and the children from Mark 10:13-16. Since the few hymns supporting this text are geared to children, she wrote "The People Came from Everywhere" as a hymn that the whole congregation could sing. It combines Jesus' warm welcome to the children with a stern message to adults.

Stanza 1 describes the crowd that gathered to hear Jesus, and incorporates rebuffs children hear today (we're busy, don't bother us).

Stanza 2 allows Jesus to express his indignation in response to the children's disappointment (a response found only in Mark's version), and suggests that Jesus gave the children the place of honor the disciples asked for later in the chapter.

Stanza 3 points to the trust of children as a model of faith for adults.

Stanza 4 is a prayer that recalls Jesus' blessing of the children and asks that our quest be similarly rewarded.

The biblical story has traditionally been used to emphasize Jesus' love and acceptance of children, and John's hymn tune, CHILD'S PLAY, suggests this joyful occasion. However, when Jesus' challenge to the faith of adults is stressed in worship, a tune such as SHEPHERD'S PIPES or CLONMEL might be considered. John has also written an anthem setting for multiple choirs that incorporates ST. FLAVIAN, along with an original melody.*

---

*"The People Came from Everywhere," Abingdon Press, #02660-1 *(Church Music for Children* Anthem Series). Unison/SATB with keyboard.

The People Came from Everywhere

1. The peo - ple came from ev - 'ry - where to
2. When Je - sus saw the chil - dren turn, their
3. "The ho - ly realm of God be - longs to
4. As once you took your hands and blessed the

hear the Teach - er's news. The
fac - es long and glum, he
chil - dren such as these, who
chil - dren on their way, now

blind, the lame, the poor were there, en -
told his friends, "When will you learn that
trust that God will right all wrongs, for -
bless us, Je - sus, in our quest to

cour - aged by his views. But
lit - tle ones must come?" He
give, and bring us peace. If
find your love, we pray. We

WORDS: Mary Nelson Keithahn
MUSIC: John D. Horman

CHILD'S PLAY
86.86.86.86.6

© 1997 Abingdon Press

those who brought the chil - dren near were quick - ly
chi - ded them in - dig - nant - ly, "God's love can't
you would al - so now re - ceive the love that
long to feel your warm em - brace, and hear your

sent a - way: "The Teach - er's far too
be de - nied! Let all the chil - dren
nev - er ends, come as a trust - ing
kind - ly word, that in the pres - ence

bus - y now. Don't both - er him to - day.
come to me and sit here at my side,
child, be - lieve in all that God in - tends,
of your grace our faith might be as - sured,

Don't both - er him to - day."
come sit here at my side."
in all that God in - tends."
our faith might be as - sured.

Your Spirit, God, Moves Us to Pray

Your Spirit, God, moves us to pray
for children in the world today
whose only home may be the street,
who never have enough to eat,
who fear the night, and dread the day,
and cannot go outside to play:
God, bless the children, let them live.
Teach our hearts and hands to give.

Your Spirit, God, moves us to pray
for children in the world today
whose tongues must learn new ways to talk,
who cannot see or hear or walk,
who toil in shops 'til hands are sore,
who mourn their loved ones lost in war:
God, bless the children, let them live.
Teach our hearts and hands to give.

Kind, gentle God, this is our prayer:
that we might learn to love and share
the blessings that you shower down—
a loving home, a friendly town,
good food to eat, warm clothes to wear,
and when we're sick, a doctor's care.
God, bless the children, let them live,
Teach our hearts and hands to give.

WORDS: Mary Nelson Keithahn
© 1996, 1997 Abingdon Press

About the Text and Tune

Live by the Spirit ... the fruit of the Spirit is love, joy, peace, patience, kindness, generosity, faithfulness, gentleness, and self-control. ... Bear one another's burdens ... whenever we have an opportunity, let us work for the good of all (Gal. 5:16a, 22; 6:2, 10).

On June 1, 1996, Mary happened to tune in CNN's live broadcast of the *Stand for the Children* march in Washington, D. C. She was so moved by the stories she heard that she wrote "Your Spirit, God, Moves Us to Pray" for use as a spoken prayer in a church school curriculum course she was revising. John set the text to a tune he named CABIN JOHN after the Potomac, Maryland school where he had taught.

The hymn reminds us that, as Christians who have received the gifts of the Spirit, we must be sensitive to the needs of children and willing to share God's blessings with them.

Stanzas 1 and 2 describe the many ways children throughout the world are treated unjustly.

Stanza 3 is a prayer asking God to help us share the blessings we enjoy.

The refrain asks God's blessing on children everywhere and prays that God will teach us how to give with our hearts and our hands.

"Your Spirit, God, Moves Us to Pray" would be appropriate for Children's Sabbath/Sunday, or at any time when justice for children is addressed.

Your Spirit, God, Moves Us to Pray

1. Your Spir-it, God, moves us to pray for
2. Your Spir-it, God, moves us to pray for
3. Kind, gen-tle God, this is our prayer: that

chil - dren in the world to - day
chil - dren in the world to - day
we might learn to love and share

whose on - ly home may be the street, who
whose tongues must learn new ways to talk, who
the bless - ings that you show - er down — a

nev - er have e - nough to eat,
can - not see or hear or walk,
lov - ing home, a friend - ly town,

WORDS: Mary Nelson Keithahn
MUSIC: John D. Horman

CABIN JOHN
88.88.88.D

© 1996, 1997 Abingdon Press

who   fear   the   night,   and   dread   the   day,   and
who   toil   in   shops   'til   hands   are   sore,   who
good   food   to   eat,   warm   clothes   to   wear,   and

can - not   go   out - side   to   play:
mourn   their   loved   ones   lost   in   war:
when   we're   sick,   a   doc - tor's   care.

Refrain

God,   bless   the chil-dren, let them   live.   Teach our

hearts   and   hands   to   give.

35

The Holy One of Israel

The Holy One of Israel
has promised wars will end;
the lion with the calf shall dwell,
and wolf a lamb befriend.
Let pruning hooks and plows be made
from battle swords and spears,
that people may be unafraid
and lay aside their fears.
Hallelujah! Hallelujah!
Pray for God's peace on the earth.

The desert will be glad and bloom,
the living water flow;
the hope of peace will banish gloom
and wash away all woe.
The blind shall see, the deaf will hear,
the speechless find a voice,
the lame shall leap now like a deer,
and everyone rejoice.
Hallelujah! Hallelujah!
Pray for God's peace on the earth.

The Holy One of Israel
will send a Prince of Peace,
a wise and mighty one, to dwell
with us, our joys increase.
With justice he will make things right
for all who suffer wrong,
and peace shall dawn at end of night
and tears be turned to song.
Hallelujah! Hallelujah!
Pray for God's peace on the earth.

WORDS: Mary Nelson Keithahn
© 1996, 1997 Abingdon Press

About the Text and Tune

The people who walked in darkness have seen a great light; those who lived in a land of deep darkness—on them light has shined (Isa. 9:2).

We adapted "The Holy One of Israel" from the last song in our musical drama, *Isaiah's Dream*, which was first performed at the 1996 Music, Art, and Drama (M.A.D.) camp at Placerville, near Rapid City, South Dakota. The hymn tune takes its name from the title of the musical.

The ideas are drawn from the visions of peace expressed by the eighth-century (B.C.E.) prophet Isaiah of Jerusalem:

> **Stanza 1** describes the "peaceable kingdom" foreseen in Isaiah 11:6-9 and Isaiah 2:2-4 (paralleled in Micah 4:1-4).
>
> **Stanza 2** gives a picture of what life will be like when the Messiah comes. It is based on Isaiah 35.
>
> **Stanza 3** tells what the Messiah will be like and what he will do to bring us peace, using the description in Isaiah 9:2, 6-7.
>
> **The refrain** was suggested by Psalm 122, but the prayer for peace was extended to include the whole earth, not just Jerusalem. The Hebrew form of "Alleluia" ("Hallelujah") was used because the hymn text is drawn from the Old Testament.

This hymn is appropriate for Advent and Christmas, as well as for any time the role of the Messiah or the prophetic vision of peace is addressed.

The Holy One of Israel

1. The Ho - ly One of Is - ra - el has prom - ised wars will end; the li - on with the calf shall dwell, and wolf a lamb be - friend. Let prun - ing hooks and plows be made from
2. The des - ert will be glad and bloom, the liv - ing wa - ter flow, the hope of peace will ban - ish gloom and wash a - way all woe. The blind shall see, the deaf will hear, the
3. The Ho - ly One of Is - ra - el will send a Prince of Peace, a wise and might - y one, to dwell with us, our joys in - crease. With jus - tice he will make things right for

WORDS: Mary Nelson Keithahn
MUSIC: John D. Horman

ISAIAH'S DREAM
86.86 D with Refrain

© 1996, 1997 Abingdon Press

bat - tle swords and spears, that peo - ple may be
speech - less find a voice, the lame shall leap now
all who suf - fer wrong, and peace shall dawn at

un - a - fraid and lay a - side their
like a deer, and ev - ery - one re -
end of night and tears be turned to

Refrain

fears.
joice.
song. Hal - le - lu - jah! Hal - le -

lu - jah! Pray for God's peace on the earth.

39

for Harrison Cole Keithahn

Spirit-Child Jesus

Spirit-child Jesus, in joyful refrain,
echoing songs over Bethlehem's plain,
what will we do when the carols all fade?
"Take up my song: Glory! Be not afraid!"

Spirit-child Jesus, in animal shed,
smiling at shepherds from strange borrowed bed,
what will we do when the manger's away?
"Take up my story and live it each day!"

Spirit-child Jesus, in starry white light,
twinkling on evergreens shiny and bright,
what will we do when the branches are shorn?
"Take up my cross that for you I have borne!"

Spirit-child Jesus, in vigilant eyes,
waiting the gift bearing Love's great surprise,
what will we do when the presents are done?
"Take up my presence, for I am God's Son!"

Spirit-child Jesus, in hot tongues of flame,
melting the candle alight in your name,
what will we do when the candle is gone?
"Take up my light! Pass it on, pass it on!"

WORDS: Mary Nelson Keithahn
© 1997 Abingdon Press

About the Text and Tune

If then there is any encouragement in Christ, any consolation from love, any sharing in the Spirit, any compassion and sympathy, make my joy complete: ... Let the same mind be in you that was in Christ Jesus (Phil. 2:1, 2, 5).

Mary wrote "Spirit-Child Jesus" while she was in Sacramento, California helping care for her new grandson, Harrison Cole Keithahn. John had asked for an anthem text that used familiar symbols of Christmas in new ways.* The theme of the hymn is that Christ is spiritually present in our Christmas traditions, calling us anew to discipleship, not just in the Christmas season, but throughout our lives.

The *carols* in **Stanza 1** tell us to trust God and not be anxious or afraid.

The *creche* in **Stanza 2** reminds us to love one another as Christ has loved us.

The lighted Christmas *tree* in **Stanza 3** anticipates the cross and calls us to bear the cost of living the way of love.

The *Christmas gifts* in **Stanza 4** make us aware of God's greatest gift, received anew each time we participate in the sacrament of Communion.

The lighted *candle* in **Stanza 5** invites us to share the good news and keep it alive.

The phrase *What will we do...*, common to all five stanzas, expresses feelings we have when someone or something we have loved is gone. It describes not only our feelings when Christmas is over, but on another level, the feelings of the disciples and Mary when Jesus was crucified, rose, and returned to call them to mission. Thus the hymn suggests Christmas, Good Friday, and Pentecost, and ends with a challenge to pass on the faith we share.

John named his tune SPIRIT-CHILD after the opening line of Stanza 1.

---

*"Spirit-Child Jesus," Abingdon Press, #08134-3 *(Church Music for Children* Anthem Series). Unison/SATB with keyboard, flute, and handbells.

Spirit-Child Jesus

1. Spir – it – child Je – sus, in joy – ful re –
2. Spir – it – child Je – sus, in an – i – mal
3. Spir – it – child Je – sus, in star – ry white
4. Spir – it – child Je – sus, in vig – i – lant
5. Spir – it – child Je – sus, in hot tongues of

frain, ech – o – ing songs o – ver
shed, smil – ing at shep – herds from
light, twin – kling on ev – er – greens,
eyes, wait – ing the gift bear – ing
flame, melt – ing the can – dle a –

Beth – le – hem's plain,
strange bor – rowed bed,
shin – y and bright,
Love's great sur – prise,
light in your name,

WORDS: Mary Nelson Keithahn
MUSIC: John D. Horman

SPIRIT-CHILD
10 10.10 10

© 1997 Abingdon Press

what	will	we	do	when	the	car - ols	all
what	will	we	do	when	the	man - ger's	a -
what	will	we	do	when	the	branch - es	are
what	will	we	do	when	the	pres - ents	are
what	will	we	do	when	the	can - dle	is

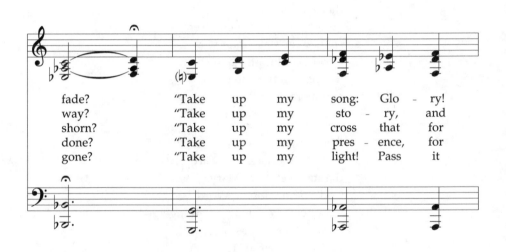

fade?	"Take	up	my	song:	Glo -	ry!
way?	"Take	up	my	sto -	ry,	and
shorn?	"Take	up	my	cross	that	for
done?	"Take	up	my	pres -	ence,	for
gone?	"Take	up	my	light!	Pass	it

Be	not	a -	fraid!"
live	it	each	day!"
you	I	have	borne!"
I	am	God's	Son!"
on,	pass	it	on!"

for Becky

As Rachel Mourned the Children

As Rachel mourned the children
King Herod said must die,
good people stood there, silent,
and no one questioned why,
why children had to suffer
to save a king his throne,
why people stood by watching
and let them die alone.

In every town and city
the Herods of our day
ignore the needs of children,
so they can have their way.
Good people still stand silent,
few dare to pay the price;
and mothers still are weeping
at each new sacrifice.

Above their cries of anguish
a child's voice can be heard,
the stable-child of Mary,
God's living, loving Word:
"Your children thirst and hunger.
Now, tell us, tell us why
you let the Herods triumph
and sentence us to die?"

Forgive us, Holy Jesus,
we did not see you there
among the countless children
committed to our care.
Stir us to break our silence
to give your love a voice,
till every weeping mother
has reason to rejoice.

WORDS: Mary Nelson Keithahn

About the Text and Tune

When Herod saw that he had been tricked by the wise men, he was infuriated, and he sent and killed all the children in and around Bethlehem who were two years old or under.... Then was fulfilled what had been spoken through the prophet Jeremiah: "A voice was heard in Ramah, wailing and loud lamentation, Rachel weeping for her children; she refused to be consoled, because they are no more" (Matt. 2:16-18).

Mary wrote "As Rachel Mourned the Children" in response to a section in *Guide My Feet*,* a book of prayers and meditations on loving and working with children written by Marian Wright Edelman, head of the Children's Defense Fund and organizer of the 1996 *Stand for the Children* march in Washington, D. C.

The inspiration for the text was Matthew's account of Herod's slaying of the innocents in Matthew 2:16-18. This is evident in **Stanzas 1 and 2.**

Stanza 3 draws on the Beatitude about those who hunger and thirst after righteousness (Matt. 5:6), and Jesus' parable of the Last Judgment (Matt. 25:40).

Stanza 4 combines a prayer of confession and a request for courage to speak out in support of children.

The minor key and impelling movement of John's tune drives home the text's challenge to be advocates for children in a world peopled with heirs to HEROD'S LEGACY. The hymn may also be sung to PASSION CHORALE.

"As Rachel Mourned the Children" is dedicated to Mary's daughter, Rebecca Umenthum, as a representative of all the teachers and parents who are investing their lives in loving and working with children. It is appropriate for Children's Sabbath/Sunday, Epiphany Sunday, or at any time when justice for children is a concern of the congregation.

*Boston: Beacon Press, 1995.

As Rachel Mourned the Children

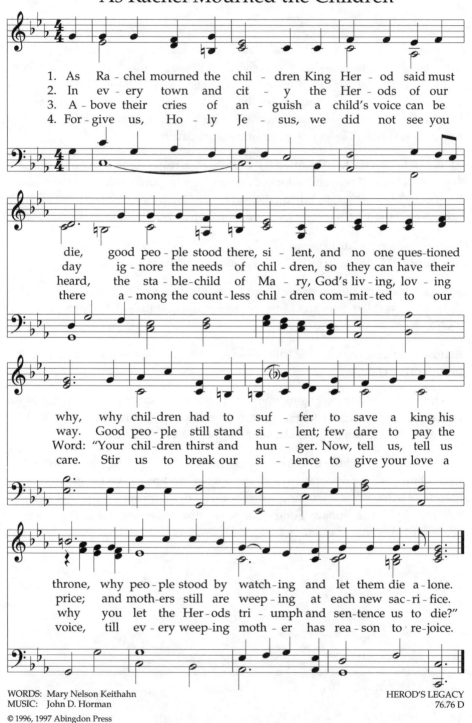

1. As Ra-chel mourned the chil-dren King Her-od said must die, good peo-ple stood there, si-lent, and no one ques-tioned why, why chil-dren had to suf-fer to save a king his throne, why peo-ple stood by watch-ing and let them die a-lone.

2. In ev-ery town and cit-y the Her-ods of our day ig-nore the needs of chil-dren, so they can have their way. Good peo-ple still stand si-lent; few dare to pay the price; and moth-ers still are weep-ing at each new sac-ri-fice.

3. A-bove their cries of an-guish a child's voice can be heard, the sta-ble-child of Ma-ry, God's liv-ing, lov-ing Word: "Your chil-dren thirst and hun-ger. Now, tell us, tell us why you let the Her-ods tri-umph and sen-tence us to die?"

4. For-give us, Ho-ly Je-sus, we did not see you there a-mong the count-less chil-dren com-mit-ted to our care. Stir us to break our si-lence to give your love a voice, till ev-ery weep-ing moth-er has rea-son to re-joice.

WORDS: Mary Nelson Keithahn
MUSIC: John D. Horman

HEROD'S LEGACY
76.76 D

© 1996, 1997 Abingdon Press

Up to the Temple One Fine Day

Up to the Temple one fine day
went one who thought he knew God's way.
This Pharisee, so tall and proud,
with arms upraised, prayed thus aloud:

"How glad I am to be unique!
I'm strong where other men are weak.
I fast and tithe at your command,
and walk with you, God, hand in hand."

Then standing humbly far away,
with no such righteous résumé,
a tax collector bowed his head,
"Forgive me, God, I've sinned," he said.

Up to the Temple one fine day
went two who thought they knew God's way,
but Jesus said, in God's true sight,
the right was wrong, the wrong was right.

God, should we come to you in pride,
remind us of our sinful side,
that all who worship in this place
might seek and find forgiving grace.

WORDS: Mary Nelson Keithahn

© 1996, 1997 Abingdon Press

About the Text and Tune

Two men went up to the temple to pray, one a Pharisee and the other a tax collector (Luke 18:10).

After searching Jesus' parables for a story that would have relevance for children as well as adults, Mary decided to write a text on Luke 18:9-14, a parable Jesus told to *some who trusted in themselves that they were righteous and regarded others with contempt.* "Up to the Temple One Fine Day" suggests that, although we are all tempted to think that we are better then others, Jesus reminds us that in God's eyes, we are all the same: sinners in need of God's forgiving love.

Stanzas 1-4 are a paraphrase of the parable, and could be pantomimed by soloists representing the two men with the choir and/or congregation singing the narrative parts.

Stanza 5 is a prayer, asking that God help us be humble as we come to worship, instead of proud, that we might seek and find God's gracious love and forgiveness. This stanza should be sung by the choirs and congregation.

John set this text to a tune he named WHEATON, after a Maryland suburb near his Silver Spring home. The hymn may also be sung to CONDITOR ALME, SIDERUM, TALLIS' CANON, or OLD 100th.

"Up to the Temple One Fine Day" is appropriate for the Sunday in Year C when this text from Luke is read, and whenever Jesus' criticism of the Pharisees and our own Pharisaical attitudes are addressed.

Up to the Temple One Fine Day

1. Up to the Tem-ple one fine day went one who thought he
2. "How glad I am to be u-nique! I'm strong where oth - er
3. Then stand-ing hum-bly far a - way, with no such righ - teous
4. Up to the Tem-ple one fine day went two who thought they
5. God, should we come to you in pride, re - mind us of our

knew God's way. This Phar - i - see, so tall and proud,
men are weak. I fast and tithe at your com-mand,
ré - su - mé, a tax col - lec - tor bowed his head,
knew God's way, but Je - sus said, in God's true sight,
sin - ful side, that all who wor-ship in this place

with arms up - raised, prayed thus a - loud:
and walk with you, God, hand in hand."
"For - give me, God, I've sinned," he said.
the right was wrong, the wrong was right.
might seek and find for - giv - ing grace.

WORDS: Mary Nelson Keithahn
MUSIC: John D. Horman

WHEATON
88.88

For Philip

We Walk Today in Darkness
(A Hymn for Advent)

We walk today in darkness,
each waiting for the light
of Love that works for justice
and seeks to make things right.
We wait, sometimes forgetting
we do not wait alone,
that others long for justice
and blessings yet unknown.

We walk today in darkness,
our purpose unfulfilled.
We do not do for others
the good that God has willed.
We do not offer kindness
to those who wait in need,
nor justice to our neighbors
in every word and deed.

We walk today in darkness,
our vain hearts filled with shame.
We follow our own footsteps
and not the Spirit's flame.
Self-love bedims our vision,
self-interests cloud our sight,
and good intentions vanish
like shadows in the night.

Lord Jesus, light our darkness,
with joy dispel our gloom.
Prepare us to receive you,
and in our lives make room
for humble, loving-kindness,
for just and honest ways,
that we might walk together
in Love-illumined days.

WORDS: Mary Nelson Keithahn
© 1996, 1997 Abingdon Press

About the Text and Tune

What does the Lord require of you but to do justice, and to love kindness, and to walk humbly with your God? (Mic. 6:8). Once you were in darkness, but now in the Lord you are light. Live as children of light—for the fruit of the light is found in all that is good and right and true (Eph. 5:8-9).

Mary wrote "We Walk Today in Darkness" as a prayer for Advent, the time in the church year for reflection and preparation for the coming of Christ. She had in mind Paul's comment as he reflected on his life (Rom. 7:19), expressed so well in the General Confession: "We have followed too much the devices and desires of our own hearts. We have offended against thy holy laws. We have left undone those things which we ought to have done, and we have done those things which we ought not to have done." These sins of *omission* and sins of *commission* are responsible for keeping us in the dark, oblivious to the light of God's love. This is the meaning of the darkness mentioned in Isaiah 9:2 and 59:9.

Stanza 1 admits that we do not always consider that others are entitled to the justice we want for ourselves.

Stanza 2 confesses that we are not the kind, just persons God created us to be.

Stanza 3 repents the self-centeredness that keeps us from carrying out our good intentions to do God's will.

Stanza 4 prays that Jesus will enter our hearts and rule our lives, enabling us to "do justice, and to love kindness, and to walk humbly with God" (Mic. 6:8). Only then will we be able to live as God intends, as "children of light" instead of "children of darkness" (Eph. 5:8).

The text is dedicated to Mary's son, Philip Keithahn, a banking executive for whom justice, honesty, and kindness are important values, not only in his business but also in all of life.

John named his tune BARDSLEY after the Rev. Dr. Graham Bardsley, his pastor at Warner Memorial Presbyterian Church in Kensington, Maryland.

We Walk Today in Darkness

1. We walk to-day in dark - ness, each
2. We walk to-day in dark - ness, our
3. We walk to-day in dark - ness, our
4. Lord Je - sus, light our dark - ness, with

wait - ing for the light of Love that works for
pur - pose un - ful - filled. We do not do for
vain hearts filled with shame. We fol - low our own
joy dis - pel our gloom. Pre - pare us to re -

jus - tice and seeks to make things right. We
oth - ers the good that God has willed. We
foot - steps and not the Spir - it's flame. Self -
ceive you, and in our lives make room for

WORDS: Mary Nelson Keithahn
MUSIC: John D. Horman

BARDSLEY
76.76 D

wait, some - times for - get - ting we do not wait a -
do not of - fer kind - ness to those who wait in
love be - dims our vi - sion, self - in - terests cloud our
hum - ble, lov - ing - kind - ness, for just and hon - est

lone, that oth - ers long for jus - tice and
need, nor jus - tice to our neigh - bors in
sight, and good in - ten - tions van - ish like
ways, that we might walk to - geth - er in

bless - ings yet un - known. _____
ev - ery word and deed. _____
shad - ows in the night. _____
Love - il - lu - mined days. _____

For Krista and her family

When It Seemed that Love Was Dying

When it seemed that Love was dying,
hope and joy forever gone,
friends of Jesus, fearful, wondered
who would help them carry on.
Joseph came to claim the body,
Nicodemus, too, was there,
bravely showing their allegiance,
handling him with tender care.

In a borrowed tomb they laid him,
breathless, broken, and alone;
then, before they left the garden,
sealed the doorway with a stone.
Women, watching, stood by weeping,
lost in sorrow, deep in gloom,
never dreaming God would bring forth
life anew from barren womb.

Sunday, when the tomb was empty,
Mary cried in great dismay,
till she heard these words of greeting:
"Jesus Christ is risen today!
Fear not! Go and tell the others:
There's no need to weep or cry.
Earth is filled with alleluias!
Hope and love will never die!"

Mary and the others found their
friends who hid in fear and grief.
"Wipe your tears and gather courage!
Hear this news beyond belief:
We have seen him! Christ is living!
God has rolled away the stone!
Alleluia! Alleluia!
Praise God! We are not alone!"

When it seemed that Love was dying,
Love showed it could rise again,
filling empty hearts with courage,
hope, and joy, a glad "Amen!"
Let us, too, be alleluias,
serving you, Lord, to the end.
Alleluia! Alleluia!
Live in us now, Risen Friend!

WORDS: Mary Nelson Keithahn

© 1997 Abingdon Press

About the Text and Tune

"Why do you look for the living among the dead? He is not here, but has risen" (Luke 24:5b).

Although this Easter text retells the story of the Resurrection in John 19:38-42 and 20:1-18, it also draws on parallel accounts in the other Gospels (Matt. 27:55-61 and 28:1-8; Mark 15:40-47; and Luke 23:44-55 and 24:1-12).

People respond to the death of a loved one in different ways. This is evident in the actions of Jesus' disciples after his crucifixion. Joseph of Arimathea and Nicodemus had not openly supported Jesus during his lifetime, they were also the ones who came forward to claim his body and arrange for his burial. Perhaps they felt guilty for not committing themselves before. Perhaps they were willing to risk their own lives for him now because he was the only one who had made life worth living. The men who had been Jesus' disciples were nowhere to be seen. They had gone into hiding, taking their fear and grief with them. It was Mary and the other women who stood vigil at the burial, weeping as they mourned the loss of their beloved teacher. None of the disciples expected they would see Jesus alive again. Yet the Resurrection happened, and the disciples were forever changed! No longer grieving and afraid, but filled with Christ's spirit, they went joyfully out into the world to live "alleluia-lives," serving God in Christ's name.

"When It Seemed that Love Was Dying" is dedictated to Krista Baker, a six-year-old chorister from Mary's congregation who was killed by a drunk driver on November 15, 1991, and to her family, whose resurrection faith has enabled them to rise from the depths of their grief to be "alleluias" in their church, school, and community.

John named his tune KRISTA'S TUNE. The name "Krista" means "Christian," so it is appropriate for a text that affirms the resurrection faith embraced by all who follow Christ. The text may also be sung to HYMN OF JOY or HYFRYDOL.

When It Seemed that Love Was Dying

1. When it seemed that Love was dy - ing,
2. In a bor - rowed tomb they laid him,
3. Sun - day, when the tomb was emp - ty,
4. Ma - ry and the oth - ers found their
5. When it seemed that Love was dy - ing,

hope and joy for - ev - er gone, friends of Je - sus,
breath - less, bro - ken, and a - lone; then, be - fore they
Ma - ry cried in great dis - may till she heard these
friends who hid in fear and grief. "Wipe your tears and
Love showed it could rise a - gain, fill - ing emp - ty

fear - ful, won - dered who would help them
left the gar - den, sealed the door - way
words of greet - ing: "Je - sus Christ is
gath - er cour - age! Hear this news be -
hearts with cour - age, hope, and joy, a

WORDS: Mary Nelson Keithahn
MUSIC: John D. Horman

KRISTA'S TUNE
87.87 D

car - ry on. Jo - seph came to claim the bod - y,
with a stone. Wo - men, watch-ing, stood by weep-ing,
risen to - day! Fear not! Go and tell the oth - ers:
yond be - lief: We have seen him! Christ is liv - ing!
glad "A - men!" Let us, too, be al - le - lu - ias,

Nic - o - de - mus, too, was there,
lost in sor - row, deep in gloom,
There's no need to weep or cry.
God has rolled a - way the stone!
serv - ing you, Lord, to the end.

brave - ly show - ing their al - le - giance,
nev - er dream - ing God would bring forth
Earth is filled with al - le - lu - ias!
Al - le - lu - ia! Al - le - lu - ia!
Al - le - lu - ia! Al - le - lu - ia!

hand - ling him with ten - der care.
life a - new from bar - ren womb.
Hope and love will nev - er die!"
Praise God! We are not a - lone!"
Live in us now, Ris - en Friend!

For my mother, Vivian Sheldon Nelson

When People Learned of Jesus Christ

When people learned of Jesus Christ,
they went to hear him preach.
They longed to find out for themselves
what Jesus had to teach.
They pondered over parables
and gave his words much thought,
but what they most remembered was
the love that Jesus taught.

He turned the water into wine
and multiplied the bread,
becalmed the heavy, stormy seas,
and even raised the dead.
The people wondered at the signs
and miracles he wrought,
but what they most remembered was
the love that Jesus taught.

He answered scribes and Pharisees
who would with him contend.
He healed the sick, the blind, the lame,
and was the sinners' friend.
They marveled at his prophecies,
the healing that he brought,
but what they most remembered was
the love that Jesus taught.

We may not work a miracle,
fulfill a prophet's role,
encourage sinners to repent,
or make the wounded whole;
but, as disciples, we can tell
we've found what all have sought:
the never-ending love of God,
the love that Jesus taught.

Dear God, at home, at work, at school,
in all of life, we pray,
help us be teachers who reveal
your love for us today,
that all the world may recognize
the Spirit that is caught
when his disciples try to live
the love that Jesus taught.

WORDS: Mary Nelson Keithahn

© 1997 Abingdon Press

About the Text and Tune

Then Jesus went about all the cities and villages, teaching in their synagogues, and proclaiming the good news of the kingdom, and curing every disease and every sickness (Matt. 9:35). *"You have one teacher, and you are all students"* (Matt. 23:8). *"Go therefore and make disciples ... teaching them to obey everything that I have commanded you"* (Matt. 28:19-20).

In 1997 the Association of Presbyterian Church Educators held a contest for a new hymn on "the ministry of education as a means to glorify and serve God." We wrote "When People Learned of Jesus Christ" as our entry. Mary's focus in the text is on Jesus as a "master teacher" and role model for us to follow. Both the friends and enemies of Jesus saw him in this way, referring to him regularly as "Teacher," despite the many other roles he played in their lives. However, although Jesus called his disciples to a ministry of teaching (Matt. 28:19-20), he reminded them that *he* was the Teacher and *they* were only students (Matt. 23:8-10). "When People Learned of Jesus Christ" explores this paradox.

Stanzas 1-3 recall Jesus' ministry of preaching, teaching, healing, and miraculous acts, but emphasize that he was remembered most for what he taught them about God's love.

Stanza 4 recognizes that although we cannot do all the wondrous things Jesus did, we can share the good news of God's love with one another as we go about the business of being a Christian community. We can be "teachers" without being the "Teacher."

Stanza 5 is a prayer asking God to help us in this task.

The text is dedicated to Mary's mother and mentor, Vivian Sheldon Nelson, who in her many years of church teaching, faithfully expressed the love that Jesus taught.

John named his tune DEDICATION, in honor of all who have been committed to the ministry of teaching in the church. The hymn may also be sung to CLONMEL, A PURPLE ROBE, SHEPHERD'S PIPES, ALL SAINTS NEW, KINGSFOLD, or FOREST GREEN.

When People Learned of Jesus Christ

1. When peo - ple learned of Je - sus Christ, they went to hear him preach. They longed to find out for them-selves what Je - sus had to teach. They
2. He turned the wat - er in - to wine and mul - ti - plied the bread, be - calmed the heav - y, storm - y seas, and e - ven raised the dead. The
3. He an - swered scribes and Phar - i - sees who would with him con - tend. He healed the sick, the blind, the lame, and was the sin - ners' friend. They
4. We may not work a mir - a - cle, ful - fill a proph - et's role, en - cour - age sin - ners to re - pent, or make the wound - ed whole; but,
5. Dear God, at home, at work, at school, in all of life, we pray, help us be teach - ers who re - veal your love for us to - day, that

*Hymn may be sung in four parts, SATB.

WORDS: Mary Nelson Keithahn
MUSIC: John D. Horman

DEDICATION
86.86 D

© 1997 Abingdon Press

pon - dered o - ver par - a - bles and gave his words much
peo - ple won - dered at the signs and mir - a - cles he
mar - veled at his proph - e - cies, the heal - ing that he
as dis - ci - ples, we can tell we've found what all have
all the world may rec - og - nize the Spir - it that is

thought, but what they most re - mem-bered was the
wrought, but what they most re - mem-bered was the
brought, but what they most re - mem-bered was the
sought: the nev - er - end - ing love of God, the
caught when his dis - ci - ples try to live the

love that Je - sus taught, the love that Je - sus taught.
love that Je - sus taught the love that Je - sus taught.
love that Je - sus taught, the love that Je - sus taught.
love that Je - sus taught, the love that Je - sus taught.
love that Je - sus taught, the love that Je - sus taught.

Come Away with Me to a Quiet Place

Come away with me to a quiet place,
apart from the world with its frantic pace,
to pray, reflect, and seek God's grace.
Come away with me. Come away.

Come and pray with me on a gentle sea,
on top of a hill in the Galilee,
in gardens like Gethsemane.
Come away with me. Come away.

Come today with thoughts of the countless ways
that God's steadfast love blesses all our days,
and join with me in silent praise.
Come away with me. Come away.

Come and say, in words whispered from your soul,
the feelings and actions you can't control.
Your spirit needs to be made whole.
Come away with me. Come away.

Come away with me to a quiet place,
to God's loving arms waiting to embrace
all those who come in hope of grace.
Come away with me. Come away.

WORDS: Mary Nelson Keithahn
© 1997 Abingdon Press

About the Text and Tune

The apostles gathered around Jesus, and told him all they had done and taught. He said to them, "Come away to a deserted place all by yourselves and rest a while." For many were coming and going, and they had no leisure even to eat. And they went away in the boat to a deserted place by themselves (Mark 6:30-32).

Mary wrote "Come Away with Me to a Quiet Place" while doing an anthem text for children on the same scripture. The hymn is an invitation to prayer.

Stanza 1 sets the theme, recalling Jesus' inviting the disciples to retreat from the world and its problems in order to rest awhile and pray (Mark 6:30-32).

Stanza 2 recalls quiet places where Jesus prayed: a deserted spot on the Sea of Galilee that he reached by boat (Matt. 14:13), a hill where he taught his disciples to pray the Lord's Prayer (Matt. 6:9-13), and the Garden of Gethsemane where he went to pray on the night he was betrayed (Matt. 26:36). We had experienced prayer in these areas ourselves when we were in Israel in 1996.

Stanza 3 suggests that prayer begins with reflection and thoughtful remembrance of God's blessings. Expressing joy in God's presence does not have to be noisy. Praise can also be quiet, even silent.

Stanza 4 invites honest confession of our need for God's help in getting our feelings and actions under control, so we can be the loving persons God intends us to be.

Stanza 5 assures us that all who come to God in prayer are welcome, and will benefit from God's gracious and steadfast love.

John named his tune RECREATION because it is as we take time out from our busy lives for rest, relaxation, and prayer that we are "re-created" to begin God's work anew. The text may also be sung to AURELIA or MUNICH.

Come Away with Me

1. Come a - way with me to a qui - et
2. Come and pray with me on a gen - tle
3. Come to - day with thoughts of the count - less
4. Come and say, in words whis - pered from your
5. Come a way with me to a qui - et

place, a - part from the world with its fran - tic pace,
sea, on top of a hill in the Gal - i - lee,
ways that God's stead - fast love bless - es all our days,
soul, the feel - ings and ac - tions you can't con - trol.
place, to God's lov - ing arms wait - ing to em - brace

to pray, re - flect, and seek God's grace.
in gar - dens like Geth - se - ma - ne.
and join with me in si - lent praise.
Your spir - it needs to be made whole.
all those who come in hope of grace.

Refrain

Come a - way with me. Come a - way.

WORDS: Mary Nelson Keithahn
MUSIC: John D. Horman

RECREATION
10 10. 8 8